The Little Book of
Olympic Spirit

More than 185 inspirational quotes from the Games

**Edited by Iain Spragg
and Adrian Clarke**

CARLTON

First published by Carlton Books Limited 2011
Copyright © 2011 Carlton Books Limited

London 2012 emblems: ™ & ® The London Organising
Committee of the Olympic Games and Paralympic Games Ltd
(LOCOG) 2007. The London 2012 Pictograms © LOCOG
2009. All Rights Reserved.

Carlton Books Limited,
20 Mortimer Street,
London, W1T 3JW.

FSC
www.fsc.org
MIX
Paper from
responsible sources
FSC® C101537

A CIP catalogue record for this book is
available from the
British Library.

10 9 8 7 6 5 4 3 2 1

ISBN: 978-1-84732-837-3

Printed in China

Bibliography includes:
David Pickering, *Great Sporting Quotations*, Past Times, 2001
Colin Jarman, *The Guinness Dictionary Of Sports Quotations*,
Guinness Publishing Ltd, 1990

Introduction

Sport's greatest global gathering, the modern Olympic Games are an unrivalled spectacle that have enthralled and enriched the world ever since Frenchman Baron Pierre de Coubertin revived the Games in 1896. This collection of thought-provoking quotes celebrates more a than a century of the movement.

From Paavo Nurmi's amazing 1,500m and 5,000m double in less than an hour at the Paris 1924 Games, to the majesty of Jesse Owens at Berlin 1936 and Bob Beamon's gravity-defying leap at Mexico 1968, right up to the record-breaking brilliance of Usain Bolt at Beijing 2008, the Olympic Games never fail to inspire and entertain in equal measure.

This compilation of quotations from some of the Olympics Games' legendary athletes and administrators commemorates the men and women who made it their life's ambition to emulate the Olympic Games motto – faster, higher, stronger.

Iain Spragg and Adrian Clarke

'The battles that count aren't the ones for gold medals. The struggles within yourself – the invisible, inevitable battles inside all of us – that's where it's at.'

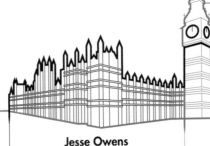

Jesse Owens
American athlete, four-time Olympic
gold medallist (Berlin 1936)

'An athlete cannot run with money in his pockets. He must run with hope in his heart and dreams in his head.'

Emil Zátopek
Czechoslovakian athlete, four-time Olympic
gold medallist (London 1948, Helsinki 1952)

'The Olympics remain the most compelling search for excellence that exists in sport, and maybe in life itself.'

Dawn Fraser
Australian swimmer, four-time Olympic
gold medallist (Melbourne 1956,
Rome 1960, Tokyo 1964)

'For athletes, the Olympics are the
ultimate test of their worth.'

Mary Lou Retton
American gymnast, Olympic gold medallist
(Los Angeles 1984)

'If you dream and you allow yourself to dream you can do anything. And that's what this Olympic medal represents.'

Clara Hughes
Canadian cyclist and speed skater, six-time Olympic medallist (Athens 1996, Salt Lake City 2002, Turin 2006, Vancouver 2010)

'I wanted no part of politics.
And I wasn't in Berlin to compete
against any one athlete. The
purpose of the Olympics, anyway,
was to do your best ... the only
victory that counts is the one
over yourself.'

Jesse Owens
American athlete, four-time Olympic
gold medallist (Berlin 1936)

'If I've learned nothing else, it's that
time and practice equal achievement.'

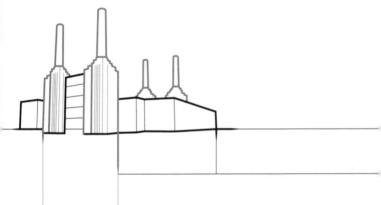

Andre Agassi
American tennis player, Olympic
gold medallist (Atlanta 1996)

'There is something in the Olympics, indefinable, springing from the soul, that must be preserved.'

Chris Brasher
British athlete, Olympic gold medallist
(Melbourne 1956)

'I keep on going because of the passion of the track. It is addictive. It's not for money, it's simply the thrill of racing.'

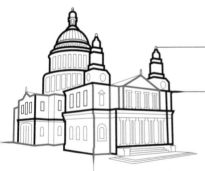

Haile Gebrselassie
Ethiopian athlete, two-time Olympic
gold medallist (Atlanta 1996, Sydney 2000)

'Never underestimate the power
of dreams and the influence of the
human spirit. We are all the same
in this notion. The potential for
greatness lives within each of us.'

Wilma Rudolph
American athlete, three-time Olympic
gold medallist (Rome 1960)

'The strength of Olympism comes to
it from that which is simply human,
hence worldwide is its essence.'

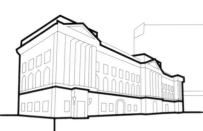

Baron Pierre de Coubertin
Founder and President of the International
Olympic Committee (1896–1925)

'Don't be afraid if things seem difficult in the beginning. That's only the initial impression. The important thing is not to retreat, you have to master yourself.'

Olga Korbut
Soviet gymnast, four-time Olympic gold medallist
(Munich 1972, Montreal 1976)

'The Olympic Movement
is a 20th century religion
where there is no injustice
of caste, of race, of
family, of wealth.'

Avery Brundage
American philanthropist and President of
the International Olympic Committee
(1952–1972)

'In 2004, I won a bronze.
This is a silver. Maybe in
2012, it will be a gold.
Slowly, slowly.'

Eliud Kipchoge
Kenyan athlete, Olympic silver medallist
(Beijing 2008)

'It seems like every day I'm in sort of a dream world. Sometimes you sort of have to pinch yourself to see if it's really real. I'm just happy I'm in the real world.'

Michael Phelps
American swimmer, 14-time
Olympic gold medallist
(Athens 2004, Beijing 2008)

'The triumph cannot be had
without the struggle. And I know
what struggle is. I have spent a
lifetime trying to share what it
has meant to be a woman first in
the world of sports so that other
young women have a chance to
reach their dreams.'

Wilma Rudolph
American athlete, three-time Olympic
gold medallist (Rome 1960)

'For all of us it's been a massive inspiration. Now looking forward to 2012, and hopefully the success the whole team has had can get the whole nation behind the Games in London.'

Ben Ainslie
British sailor, three-time Olympic gold medallist (Sydney 2000, Athens 2004, Beijing 2008)

'Be very strong and be very
methodical in your life if you want
to be a champion.'

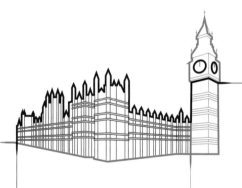

Alberto Juantorena
Cuban athlete, two-time Olympic gold
medallist (Montreal 1976)

'Winning is great, sure, but if you are really going to do something in life, the secret is learning how to lose. Nobody goes undefeated all the time. If you can pick up after a crushing defeat, and go on to win again, you are going to be a champion someday.'

Wilma Rudolph
American athlete, three-time Olympic gold medallist (Rome 1960)

'The Olympics are always a special competition. It is very difficult to predict what will happen.'

Sergei Bubka
Soviet pole vaulter, Olympic gold medallist (Seoul 1988)

'Ingenuity plus courage plus work
equals miracles.'

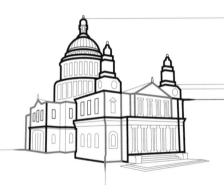

Bob Richards
American pole vaulter,
two-time Olympic gold medallist
(Helsinki 1952, Melbourne 1956)

'A trophy carries dust.
Memories last forever.'

Mary Lou Retton
American gymnast, Olympic gold medallist
(Los Angeles 1984)

'In the Olympic Oath, I ask for only one thing: sporting loyalty.'

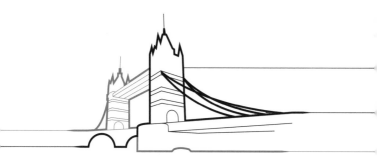

Baron Pierre de Coubertin
Founder and President of the International
Olympic Committee (1896–1925)

'Pressure is nothing
more than the shadow
of great opportunity.'

Michael Johnson
American athlete, four-time Olympic gold medallist
(Barcelona 1992, Atlanta 1996, Sydney 2000)

'It is the inspiration of the Olympic Games that drives people not only to compete but to improve and to bring lasting spiritual and moral benefits to the athlete and inspiration to those lucky enough to witness the athletic dedication.'

Herb Elliott
Australian athlete, Olympic
gold medallist (Rome 1960)

'The Olympic Games and the
Olympic Movement are about fine
athletics and fine art.'

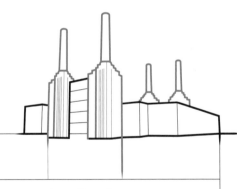

Avery Brundage
American philanthropist and President of the
International Olympic Committee (1952–1972)

'An Olympic medal is the greatest achievement and honour that can be received by an athlete. I would swap any world title to have won gold at the Olympics.'

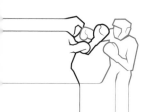

Jeff Fenech
Australian boxer
(Los Angeles 1984)

'Racing teaches us to
challenge ourselves. It teaches
us to push beyond where we
thought we could go. It helps
us to find out what we are
made of. This is what we do.
This is what it's all about.'

PattiSue Plumer
American athlete
(Seoul 1988, Barcelona 1992)

'May joy and good fellowship reign, and in this manner, may the Olympic Torch pursue its way through ages, increasing friendly understanding among nations, for the good of a humanity always more enthusiastic, more courageous and more pure.'

Baron Pierre de Coubertin
Founder and President of the International
Olympic Committee (1896–1925)

'We all have dreams. But in order to make dreams come into reality, it takes an awful lot of determination, dedication, self-discipline, and effort.'

Jesse Owens
American athlete, four-time Olympic gold medallist (Berlin 1936)

'The medals don't mean anything and the glory doesn't last. It's all about your happiness. The rewards are going to come, but my happiness is just loving the sport and having fun performing.'

Jackie Joyner-Kersee
American athlete, three-time Olympic gold medallist (Seoul 1988, Barcelona 1992)

'You can't climb up to the second floor without a ladder. When you set your aim too high and don't fulfil it, then your enthusiasm turns to bitterness. Try for a goal that's reasonable and then gradually raise it. That's the only way to get to the top.'

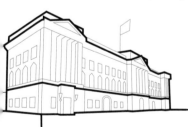

Emil Zátopek
Czechoslovakian athlete, four-time Olympic
gold medallist (London 1948, Helsinki 1952)

'I would rather have won this race
than be President of the United States.'

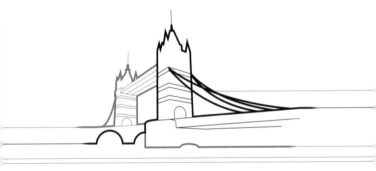

Thomas Hicks
American athlete, Olympic gold medallist
(St Louis 1904)

'The greatest memory for me of the 1984 Olympics was not the individual honours but standing on the podium with my teammates to receive our team gold medal.'

Mitch Gaylord
American gymnast,
Olympic gold medallist
(Los Angeles 1984)

'One of the great lessons I've learned in athletics is that you've got to discipline your life. No matter how good you may be, you've got to be willing to cut out of your life those things that keep you from going to the top.'

Bob Richards
American pole vaulter, two-time Olympic gold medallist (Helsinki 1952, Melbourne 1956)

'Never put an age
limit on your dreams.'

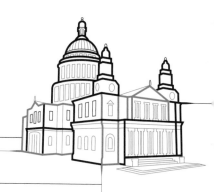

Dara Torres
American swimmer, four-time Olympic
gold medallist (Los Angeles 1984,
Barcelona 1992, Sydney 2000)

'When we stage the Olympics it will inspire kids all over the country. A kid in Scotland or Ireland will be encouraged to take up sport.'

Daley Thompson
British athlete, two-time Olympic gold medallist (Moscow 1980, Los Angeles 1984) on London 2012

'Not many people in
this world can say, "I'm an
Olympic gold medallist."'

Michael Phelps
American swimmer, 14-time Olympic gold
medallist (Athens 2004, Beijing 2008)

'The six colours, including the white background, represent the colours of all the world's flags. This is a true international emblem.'

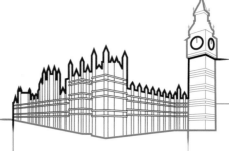

Baron Pierre de Coubertin
Founder and President of the
International Olympic Committee
(1896–1925)

'People could see in
me who I am now, an
Olympic champion, the
best in the world.'

Cathy Freeman
Australian athlete,
Olympic gold medallist
(Sydney 2000)

'The fans and supporters are also
part of the Olympic family.'

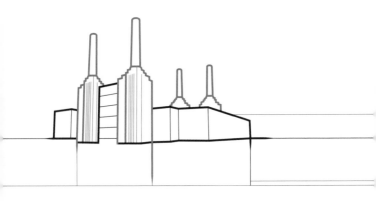

Bill Toomey
American athlete, Olympic gold medallist
(Mexico 1968)

'In the 1972 Olympic
Games, I wasn't really
going to be a star and
overnight I became a star.'

Olga Korbut
Soviet gymnast, four-time Olympic gold medallist
(Munich 1972, Montreal 1976)

'As a teenager I had no idea
that I had the potential to win
an Olympic gold medal and my
athletic career developed only by
lucky circumstances.'

Peter Snell
New Zealand athlete, three-time Olympic
gold medallist (Rome 1960, Tokyo 1964)

'Getting to know athletes from all over the planet is a big part of the Olympic experience.'

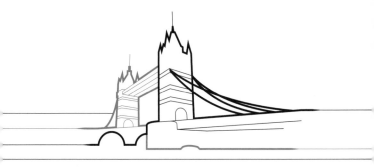

Mary Lou Retton
American gymnast, Olympic gold medallist (Los Angeles 1984)

'The feeling of accomplishment welled up inside of me, three Olympic gold medals. I knew that was something nobody could ever take away from me, ever.'

Wilma Rudolph
American athlete, three-time Olympic
gold medallist (Rome 1960)

'The most important thing in the
Olympic Games is not winning but
taking part. The essential thing in life
is not conquering but fighting well.'

Baron Pierre de Coubertin
Founder and President of the International
Olympic Committee (1896–1925)

49

'To anyone who has started out on a long campaign believing that the gold medal was destined for him, the feeling when, all of a sudden, the medal has gone somewhere else is quite indescribable.'

Sebastian Coe
British athlete, two-time Olympic gold
medallist (Moscow 1980, Los Angeles 1984)

'I didn't train to make the Olympic team until 1968. I simply trained for the moment. I never even imagined I would be an Olympic athlete. It always seemed to evolve.'

Dick Fosbury
American high jumper, Olympic gold medallist
(Mexico 1968)

'There is nothing
like the Olympics.'

HRH Princess Anne
British equestrian rider
(Montreal 1976)

'Winning is not the aim, only a
part of the whole.'

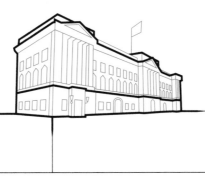

Carl Lewis
American athlete, nine-time Olympic gold
medallist (Los Angeles 1984, Seoul 1988,
Barcelona 1992, Atlanta 1996)

'It may sound strange, but many champions are made champions by setbacks.'

Bob Richards
American pole vaulter,
two-time Olympic gold medallist
(Helsinki 1952, Melbourne 1956)

'I always thought it would be neat
to make the Olympic team.'

Michael Phelps
American swimmer, 14-time Olympic gold
medallist (Athens 2004, Beijing 2008)

'The Olympic Games is the ultimate level of competition.'

Russell Mark
Australian shooter, Olympic gold medallist
(Atlanta 1996)

'I love gymnastics because I love to fly.'

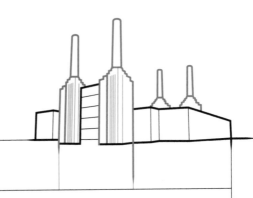

Yuriy Titov
Russian gymnast, Olympic gold medallist
(Melbourne 1956)

'The Olympic Games must not be an end in itself, they must be a means of creating a vast programme of physical education and sports competitions for all young people.'

Avery Brundage
American philanthropist and President of
the International Olympic Committee
(1952–1972)

'Winning a medal is what every
athlete dreams of and if it is the
Olympic gold, then that is the
icing on the cake.'

Jeff Fenech
Australian boxer
(Los Angeles 1984)

'What I can tell them is the way you become an Olympic champion is to start working now. I tell them why it's always worth it to put the time and effort into something you want to be good at.'

Rafer Johnson
American athlete, Olympic gold medallist
(Rome 1960)

'Sport has to remain sport, a
concept rooted on the track and
not in the balance sheet.'

Sebastian Coe
British athlete, two-time Olympic gold medallist
(Moscow 1980, Los Angeles 1984)

'The Olympic Games are for the world and all nations must be admitted to them.'

Baron Pierre de Coubertin
Founder and President of the
International Olympic Committee
(1896–1925)

'To compete in the Olympic
Games has always been
a dream. The opportunity
I have to represent
my country at them is
unbelievably exciting.'

David Beard
Australian volleyball player
(Sydney 2000, Athens 2004)

'Apart from being born, this is the greatest moment of my life.'

Jeremy Wariner
American athlete, three-time Olympic gold medallist (Athens 2004, Beijing 2008), after winning gold in the 400m at Athens 2004

'Walking into the Olympic
stadium at the Opening
Ceremony of my first Olympic
Games is a moment that I will
never forget.'

Steve Kettner
Australian weightlifter (Barcelona 1992, Atlanta 1996)

'People ask me what was going through your mind in the race? And I don't know. I try and let my body do what it knows.'

Ian Thorpe
Australian swimmer, five-time Olympic gold medallist (Sydney 2000, Athens 2004)

'Great is the victory, but the friendship of all is greater.'

Emil Zátopek
Czechoslovakian athlete, four-time Olympic gold
medallist (London 1948, Helsinki 1952)

'I was told over and over again
that I would never be successful,
that I was not going to be
competitive and the technique
was simply not going to work.
All I could do was shrug and say,
"We'll just have to see."'

Dick Fosbury
American high jumper, Olympic gold medallist
(Mexico 1968), on his new technique

'All Olympic champions are
people who believe in themselves,
and therefore in the extra power
built into personality.'

Bob Richards
American pole vaulter, two-time Olympic gold
medallist (Helsinki 1952, Melbourne 1956)

'I learned that the only way you are going to get anywhere in life is to work hard at it. Whether you're a musician, a writer, an athlete or a businessman, there is no getting around it. If you do, you'll win. If you don't, you won't.'

Bruce Jenner
American athlete, Olympic gold medallist
(Montreal 1976)

'The human body can do so much. Then the heart and soul must take over.'

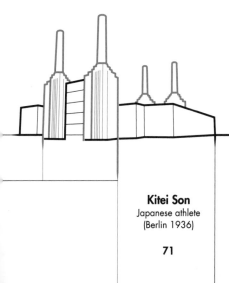

Kitei Son
Japanese athlete
(Berlin 1936)

71

'Some people say I have attitude, maybe I do, but I think you have to. You have to believe in yourself when no one else does. That makes you a winner right there.'

Venus Williams
American tennis player, three-time Olympic gold medallist (Sydney 2000, Beijing 2008)

'For success, first athletes must have talent. Second they must work and, third, they must have control of mind.'

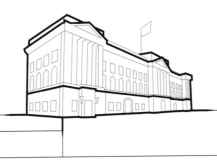

Valery Borzov
Soviet athlete, two-time Olympic gold medallist
(Munich 1972)

'The feeling of running fast is unforgettable, the exhilaration you feel running around a bend, it's like you're in charge, you're a Ferrari.'

Allan Wells
British athlete, Olympic gold medallist
(Moscow 1980)

london

'The difference between me and other athletes who go to the Olympics is that I go to win and they go to compete.'

David Bedford
British athlete (Munich 1972)

'And if we thrive, promise them
such rewards as victors wear at
the Olympic Games.'

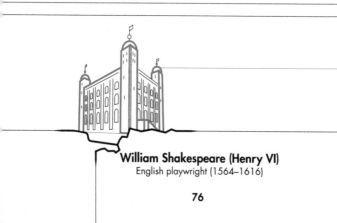

William Shakespeare (Henry VI)
English playwright (1564–1616)

'This is the college of boxing. The kind of degree you get depends on how far you go. If you win the Olympics, you get a doctorate.'

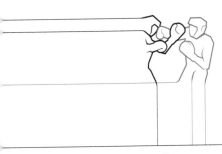

Tyrell Biggs
American boxer, Olympic gold medallist
(Los Angeles 1984)

'Standing water and a man that does not move are the same. You must move otherwise you are bound for the grave.'

Paavo Nurmi
Finnish athlete, nine-time Olympic gold medallist (Antwerp 1920, Paris 1924, Amsterdam 1928)

'If you have worked harder
enough to render yourself worthy
of going to Olympia, if you have
not been idle or ill-disciplined,
then go with confidence. But
those who have not trained in this
fashion, go where they will.'

Philostratus
Greek philosopher (c. 170–247AD)

'I came out here to beat everybody in sight and that is exactly what I'm going to do. Sure, I can do anything.'

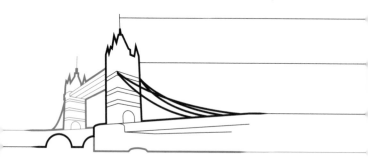

Mildred 'Babe' Didrikson

American athlete, two-time Olympic gold medallist (Los Angeles 1932)

'Behind every good decathlete,
there's a good doctor.'

Bill Toomey
American athlete, Olympic gold medallist
(Mexico 1968)

'Holding an Olympic Games
means evoking history.'

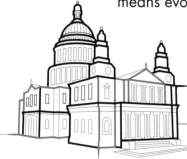

Baron Pierre de Coubertin
Founder and President of the International
Olympic Committee (1896–1925)

82

'You don't run 26 miles at five
minutes a mile on good looks and
a secret recipe.'

Frank Shorter
American athlete,
Olympic gold medallist
(Munich 1972)

'Fencing is like playing
chess with a sword in
your hand.'

Valentina Sidorova
Soviet fencer, Olympic gold medallist
(Montreal 1976)

'I was born that way, it was myself. I was gifted, that's all.'

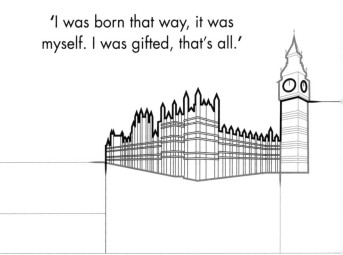

Nadia Comaneci
Romanian gymnast, five-time Olympic gold
medallist (Montreal 1976, Moscow 1980)

'If there had not been a thing as gymnastics, I would have had to invent it because I feel at one with the sport.'

Olga Korbut
Soviet gymnast, four-time
Olympic gold medallist
(Munich 1972, Montreal 1976)

'The sun warms more than
any lesser star and no festival
outshines Olympia.'

Pindar
Greek poet
(c. 522–443 BC)

'It's the getting there that counts, not
the cheese at the end of the maze.'

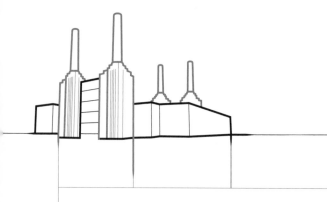

Matt Biondi
American swimmer, eight-time Olympic
gold medallist (Los Angeles 1984,
Seoul 1988, Barcelona 1992)

'I have my fun and I think I'm a
better swimmer because of it.'

Dawn Fraser
Australian swimmer, four-time Olympic
gold medallist (Melbourne 1956,
Rome 1960, Tokyo 1964)

'Olympism is not a system,
it is a state of mind.'

Baron Pierre de Coubertin
Founder and President of the International
Olympic Committee (1896–1925)

'If you can't win fairly,
you don't deserve to win.'

Steele Bishop
Australian cyclist (Munich 1972)

'Two things I felt I had to prove as a young woman in the post-war period. One that I was feminine and an athlete, and the other I was intelligent and an athlete.'

Shirley de la Hunty
Australian athlete, three-time Olympic gold medallist (Helsinki 1952, Melbourne 1956)

'I sometimes think that running has given me a glimpse of the greatest freedom a man can ever know because it results in the simultaneous liberation of both body and mind.'

Sir Roger Bannister
British athlete (Helsinki 1952)

'They don't give you gold medals for beating somebody. They give you gold medals for beating everybody.'

Michael Johnson
American athlete, four-time Olympic gold medallist
(Barcelona 1992, Atlanta 1996, Sydney 2000)

'The potential for greatness
lives within each of us.'

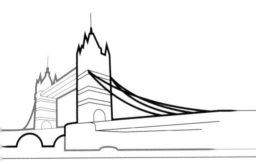

Wilma Rudolph
American athlete, three-time Olympic
gold medallist (Rome 1960)

'Lots of people let it go by and never accomplish what they want. I just wanted to see what I could do.'

Ed Moses
American athlete, two-time Olympic gold medallist (Montreal 1976, Los Angeles 1984)

'I think it will take a few days before I realise I'm Olympic champion. But this is, for sure, the biggest moment in my career, in my life. I will never forget this moment.'

Elena Dementieva
Russian tennis player, Olympic gold medallist
(Beijing 2008)

'Channel your energy. Focus.'

Carl Lewis
American athlete, nine-time Olympic gold
medallist (Los Angeles 1984, Seoul 1988,
Barcelona 1992, Atlanta 1996)

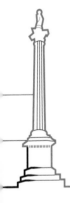

'We are different, in
essence, from other men. If
you want to win something,
run 100 metres. If you want
to experience something,
run a marathon.'

Emil Zátopek
Czechoslovakian athlete, four-time Olympic gold
medallist (London 1948, Helsinki 1952)

'Friendships are born on the field of athletic strife and the real gold of competition. Awards become corroded, friends gather no dust.'

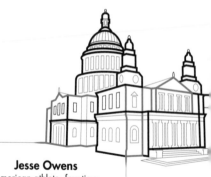

Jesse Owens
American athlete, four-time
Olympic gold medallist
(Berlin 1936)

'As a sportsman, I accept being beaten. Everybody tries to be a winner but only one in a race will win. It's fun to win. But I don't find unhappiness if I lose.'

Kip Keino
Kenyan athlete, two-time Olympic gold medallist
(Mexico 1968, Munich 1972)

'Mind is everything.
Muscle, pieces of rubber.
All that I am, I am because
of my mind.'

Paavo Nurmi
Finnish athlete, nine-time Olympic gold medallist
(Antwerp 1920, Paris 1924, Amsterdam 1928)

'Blink and you miss a sprint. The 10,000
metres is lap after lap of waiting.
Theatrically, the mile is just the right length –
beginning, middle, end, a story unfolding.'

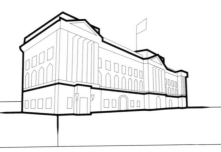

Sebastian Coe
British athlete, two-time Olympic gold medallist
(Moscow 1980, Los Angeles 1984)

'You came to this world with nothing
and will be leaving with nothing.'

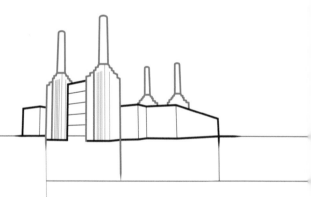

Kip Keino
Kenyan athlete, two-time Olympic gold
medallist (Mexico 1968, Munich 1972)

'Whatever you do,
don't do it halfway.'

Bob Beamon
American long jumper,
Olympic gold medallist
(Mexico 1968)

'To exercise at or near
capacity is the best way
I know of reaching a true
introspective state. If you do
it right, it can open all kinds
of inner doors.'

Al Oerter
American discus thrower, four-time Olympic
gold medallist (Melbourne 1956, Rome
1960, Tokyo 1964, Mexico 1968)

'It made me proud to know
I had been able to bring joy
into people's lives.'

Fanny Blankers-Koen
Dutch athlete, four-time Olympic gold medallist
(London 1948)

'Life is true to form, records are
meant to be broken.'

Mark Spitz
American swimmer, nine-time
Olympic gold medallist
(Mexico 1968, Munich 1972)

'It's not always a bed
of roses, but the blend
of characters makes the
strength of the team.'

Steve Redgrave
British rower, five-time Olympic
gold medallist (Los Angeles 1984,
Seoul 1988, Barcelona 1992,
Atlanta 1996, Sydney 2000)

'Training gives us an outlet for suppressed energies created by stress and thus tone the spirit just as exercise conditions the body.'

Usain Bolt
Jamaican athlete, three-time Olympic
gold medallist (Beijing 2008)

'I'm the type of guy who fails
and fails and fails, and then,
as if failure has become sick
of him, succeeds.'

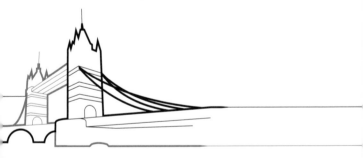

Bruce Jenner
American athlete, Olympic gold medallist
(Montreal 1976)

'You got to try and reach for the stars
or try and achieve the unreachable.'

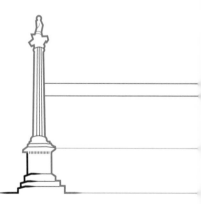

Cathy Freeman
Australian athlete, Olympic gold medallist
(Sydney 2000)

'To be part of that winning team and standing in the ring for the final decision to be announced is something I will live with for the rest of my life.'

Grahame Cheney
Australian boxer, Olympic silver medallist
(Seoul 1988)

'I can feel the wind go by when I run. It feels good. It feels fast.'

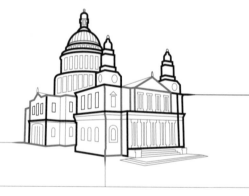

Evelyn Ashford
American athlete, four-time Olympic gold
medallist (Los Angeles 1984, Seoul 1988,
Barcelona 1992)

'I wouldn't say anything is impossible. I think that everything is possible as long as you put your mind to it and put the work and time into it.'

Michael Phelps
American swimmer, 14-time Olympic gold medallist (Athens 2004, Beijing 2008)

115

'Enjoy the journey, enjoy every moment and quit worrying about winning and losing.'

Matt Biondi
American swimmer, eight-time Olympic gold medallist (Los Angeles 1984, Seoul 1988, Barcelona 1992)

'You find out a lot about yourself through athletics. If you're cut out to be a winner or a failure or a quitter, athletics will bring it out of you. You're always stripping yourself down to the bones of your personality. And sometimes you just get a glimpse of the kind of talent you've been given. Sometimes I run and I don't even feel the effort of running. I don't even feel the ground. I'm just drifting.'

Steve Ovett
British athlete, Olympic gold medallist (Moscow 1980)

'To be number one, you have to train like you're number two.'

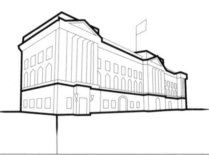

Maurice Greene
American athlete, two-time Olympic gold
medallist (Sydney 2000)

118

'Being a decathlete is like
having 10 girlfriends. You
have to love them all and you
can't afford losing one.'

Daley Thompson
British athlete, two-time Olympic gold medallist
(Moscow 1980, Los Angeles 1984)

'I don't really see the hurdles. I sense them like a memory.'

Ed Moses
American athlete, two-time Olympic gold medallist (Montreal 1976, Los Angeles 1984)

'I was pushed by myself because I have my own rule and that is that every day I run faster and try harder.'

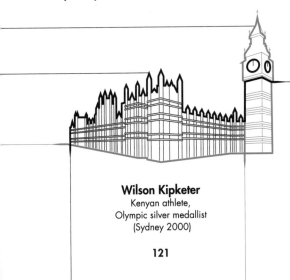

Wilson Kipketer
Kenyan athlete,
Olympic silver medallist
(Sydney 2000)

'I was 12 when I started and 34 before I achieved my dream. That should give people hope.'

Kelly Holmes
British athlete, two-time Olympic
gold medallist (Athens 2004)

'Not in my best dreams could I have imagined this.'

Rafael Nadal
Spanish tennis player,
Olympic gold medallist (Beijing 2008)

'They may become harder to achieve but your dreams can't stop because you've hit a certain age or you've had a child.'

Dara Torres
American swimmer, four-time Olympic gold medallist (Los Angeles 1984, Barcelona 1992, Sydney 2000)

'I concentrate on preparing to swim
my race and let the other swimmers
think about me, not me about them.'

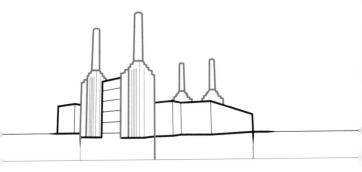

Amanda Beard
American swimmer, two-time Olympic gold
medallist (Atlanta 1996, Athens 2004)

'Olympism is a doctrine of the fraternity
between the body and the soul.'

Baron Pierre de Coubertin
Founder and President of the International
Olympic Committee (1896–1925)

'I always loved running, it was something you could do by yourself and under your own power. You could go in any direction, fast or slow as you wanted, fighting the wind if you felt like it, seeking out new sights just on the strength of your feet and the courage of your lungs.'

Jesse Owens
American athlete, four-time Olympic gold medallist (Berlin 1936)

'The memories of the Munich games
for me are of triumph and tragedy.'

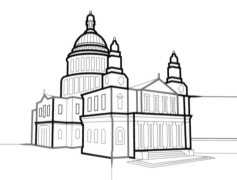

Mark Spitz
American swimmer, nine-time
Olympic gold medallist
(Mexico 1968, Munich 1972)

'Remember these six minutes for the rest of your lives. Listen to the crowd and take it all in. This is the stuff of dreams.'

Steve Redgrave
British rower, five-time Olympic gold medallist
(Los Angeles 1984, Seoul 1988, Barcelona 1992,
Atlanta 1996, Sydney 2000)

'You have to wonder at times
what you're doing out there.
Over the years, I've given myself
a thousand reasons to keep
running, but it always comes back
to where it started. It comes down
to self-satisfaction and a sense of
achievement.'

Steve Prefontaine
American athlete (Munich 1972)

'I felt a huge sense of relief after winning Olympic silver. That's it over. I've done it. I'm not going to spend my life looking back, the sportsman's nightmare.'

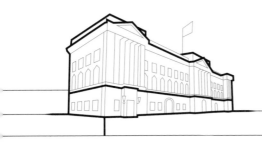

Roger Black
British athlete, two-time Olympic
silver medallist (Atlanta 1996)

131

'You can't put a limit on anything.'

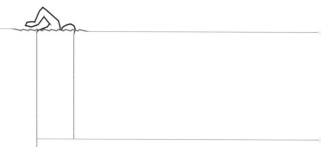

Michael Phelps
American swimmer, 14-time
Olympic gold medallist
(Athens 2004, Beijing 2008)

'The only way to overcome is to hang in.'

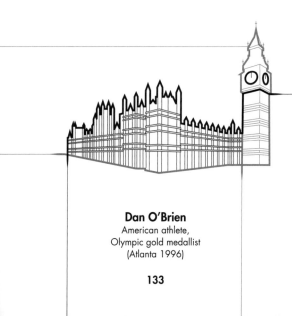

Dan O'Brien
American athlete,
Olympic gold medallist
(Atlanta 1996)

133

'To describe the agony of a marathon to somebody who's never run it is like trying to explain colour to a person who was born blind.'

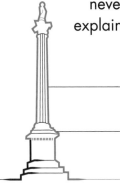

Jerome Drayton
Canadian athlete (Montreal 1976)

'Scientists have proven that it's impossible to long-jump 30 feet but I don't listen to that kind of talk. Thoughts like that have a way of sinking into your feet.'

Carl Lewis
American athlete, nine-time Olympic gold medallist (Los Angeles 1984, Seoul 1988, Barcelona 1992, Atlanta 1996)

'I have long believed that athletic
competition among people and nations
should replace violence and wars.'

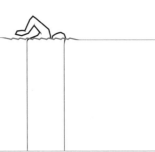

Johnny Weissmuller
American swimmer, five-time Olympic gold
medallist (Paris 1924, Amsterdam 1928)

'The Olympic Games were
created for the exaltation of the
individual athlete.'

Baron Pierre de Coubertin
Founder and President of the International
Olympic Committee (1896–1925)

'God made me fast. And when I
run, I feel His pleasure.'

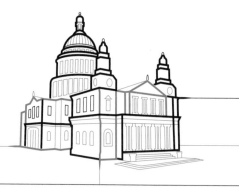

Eric Liddell
British athlete, Olympic gold medallist (Paris 1924)

'Gold medals aren't really made of gold. They're made of sweat, determination and a hard-to-find alloy called guts.'

Dan Gable
American wrestler,
Olympic gold medallist
(Munich 1972)

'Olympism is the marriage of
sport and culture.'

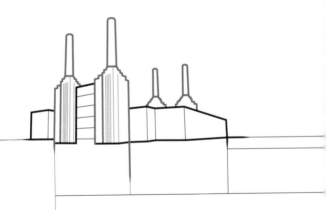

Juan Antonio Samaranch
President of the International Olympic
Committee (1980–2001)

'To give anything less than your best is to sacrifice the Gift.'

Steve Prefontaine
American athlete (Munich 1972)

'When you cross the line, it is such a wonderful feeling it's hard to describe.'

Kelly Holmes
British athlete, two-time Olympic gold medallist (Athens 2004)

'Being your best is not so much about overcoming the barriers other people place in front of you as it is about overcoming the barriers we place in front of ourselves. It has nothing to do with how many times you win or lose. It has no relation to where you finish in a race or whether you break world records. But it does have everything to do with having the vision to dream, the courage to recover from adversity and the determination never to be shifted from your goals.'

Kieren Perkins
Australian swimmer, two-time Olympic gold
medallist (Barcelona 1992, Atlanta 1996)

'The water is your friend. You don't have to fight with water, just share the same spirit as the water, and it will help you move.'

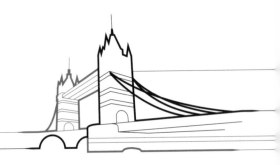

Aleksandr Popov
Russian swimmer, four-time Olympic gold medallist
(Barcelona 1992, Atlanta 1996)

'Chance can allow you to
accomplish a goal every
once in a while but consistent
achievement happens only if you
love what you are doing.'

Bart Conner
American gymnast, two-time Olympic
gold medallist (Los Angeles 1984)

'For myself, losing is not coming second. It's getting out of the water knowing you could have done better. For myself, I have won every race I've been in.'

Ian Thorpe
Australian swimmer, five-time Olympic gold medallist (Sydney 2000, Athens 2004)

'Mental will is a muscle that needs
exercise, just like muscles of
the body.'

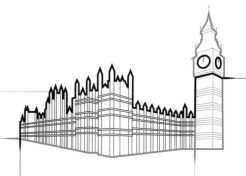

Lynn Jennings
American athlete,
Olympic bronze medallist
(Barcelona 1992)

147

'I'm very determined and stubborn. There's a desire in me that makes me want to do more and more and to do it right. Each one of us has a fire in our heart for something. It's our goal in life to find it and to keep it lit.'

Mary Lou Retton
American gymnast, Olympic gold medallist
(Los Angeles 1984)

'Find the good. It's all around
you. Find it, showcase it and
you'll start believing in it.'

Jesse Owens
American athlete, four-time Olympic
gold medallist (Berlin 1936)

'My Olympic voyage has continued
because it is so rewarding.'

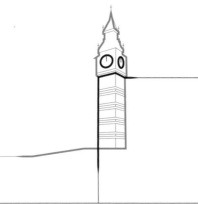

Bill Toomey
American athlete, Olympic gold medallist
(Mexico 1968)

'You have to forget your last marathon before you try another. Your mind can't know what's coming.'

Frank Shorter
American athlete, Olympic gold medallist
(Munich 1972)

'A lot of people run a race to see who's the fastest. I run to see who has the most guts.'

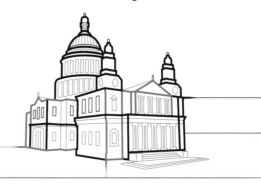

Steve Prefontaine
American athlete (Munich 1972)

'If a young female sees my dreams and goals come true, they will realise their dreams and goals might also come true.'

Jackie Joyner-Kersee
American athlete, three-time Olympic gold
medallist (Seoul 1988, Barcelona 1992)

'All of my life I have always had the urge to do things better than anybody else.'

Mildred 'Babe' Didrikson
American athlete, two-time Olympic gold
medallist (Los Angeles 1932)

'I believe in God. He is the
secret of my success. He gives
people talent.'

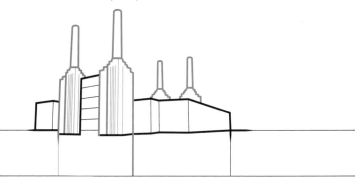

Noureddine Morceli
Algerian athlete, Olympic gold medallist
(Atlanta 1996)

'The thrill of competing carries with it the thrill of a gold medal. One wants to win to prove himself the best.'

Jesse Owens
American athlete, four-time Olympic gold medallist (Berlin 1936)

'I was nearly sick. But that's how you have to ride, as if you never want to breathe again.'

Emma Pooley
British cyclist, Olympic silver medallist
(Beijing 2008)

'Winning has always meant much to me,
but winning friends has meant the most.'

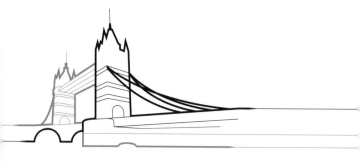

Mildred 'Babe' Didrikson
American athlete, two-time Olympic
gold medallist (Los Angeles 1932)

158

'In sports, people reach their peak very early. You have to move on. I don't know if I will ever surpass what I did at the Olympics, but I'm still doing the work I always wanted to do.'

Greg Louganis
American diver, four-time Olympic gold medallist
(Los Angeles 1984, Seoul 1988)

'The glory of sport comes from dedication, determination and desire. Achieving success and personal glory in athletics has less to do with wins and losses than it does with learning how to prepare yourself so that at the end of the day, whether on the track or in the office, you know that there was nothing more you could have done to reach your ultimate goal.'

Jackie Joyner-Kersee
American athlete, three-time Olympic gold medallist (Seoul 1988, Barcelona 1992)

'I've dreamed about this a thousand times, to see those silver medals in my bedroom turn into gold.'

Zhang Juanjuan
South Korean archer, Olympic gold medallist
(Beijing 2008)

'I caught the Olympic vision when I was 10 years old. Watching the 1972 Games on television was when I fully understood what the Olympics was all about and what the highest accomplishment was in the sport of wrestling. I knew at 10 I wanted to be an Olympic gold medallist and to be the best in the world.'

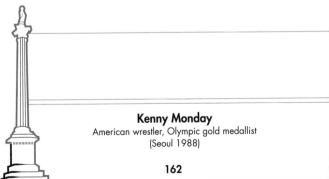

Kenny Monday
American wrestler, Olympic gold medallist
(Seoul 1988)

162

'The pain shot through me like a
knife. It brought tears to my eyes.
But now I have a gold medal and
the pain is gone.'

Shun Fujimoto
Japanese gymnast, Olympic gold medallist
(Montreal 1976)

'All pressure is self-inflicted. It's what you make of it or how you let it rub off on you.'

Sebastian Coe
British athlete, two-time
Olympic gold medallist
(Moscow 1980, Los Angeles 1984)

'Now I am not comparing this to what a soldier goes through in war or what a police officer is at times faced with, but I will tell you, as for sport, nothing compares to the Olympic Games as far as pressure is concerned. Some things may be equal to it but nothing surpasses it.'

Lanny Bassham
American shooter, Olympic gold medallist
(Montreal 1976)

'I like added pressure. It makes me work harder.'

Mary Lou Retton
American gymnast, Olympic gold medallist
(Los Angeles 1984)

'Tomorrow is another day, and there will be another battle.'

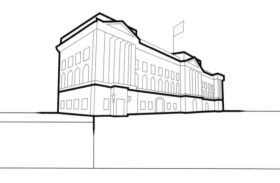

Sebastian Coe
British athlete, two-time Olympic gold medallist
(Moscow 1980, Los Angeles 1984)

'If you want to become the best runner you can be, start now. Don't spend the rest of your life wondering if you can do it.'

Priscilla Welch
British athlete (Los Angeles 1984)

'Go into the sport because you have fun doing it, not because of "what ifs" and dreams of gold medals. That way, no matter what happens, you win.'

Shannon Miller
American gymnast, two-time Olympic gold medallist (Atlanta 1996)

'Some people create with words or with music or with a brush and paints. I like to make something beautiful when I run. I like to make people stop and say, "I've never seen anyone run like that before." It's more than just a race, it's a style. It's doing something better than anyone else. It's being creative.'

Steve Prefontaine
American athlete (Munich 1972)

'The most important thing I've done in my life was winning the Olympic gold medal for my mother.'

Oscar de la Hoya
American boxer, Olympic gold medallist
(Barcelona 1992)

london

'I am building a fire, and every day I train, I add more fuel. At just the right moment, I light the match.'

Mia Hamm
American footballer, two-time
Olympic gold medallist
(Atlanta 1996, Athens 2004)

'I run to be known as the greatest runner, the greatest of all time. I could not eat or sleep for a week after I lost in the 1992 Olympics. I have to win or die.'

Noureddine Morceli
Algerian athlete, Olympic gold medallist
(Atlanta 1996)

'Boxing is the ultimate challenge.
There's nothing that can compare
to testing yourself the way you do
every time you step in the ring.'

Sugar Ray Leonard
American boxer,
Olympic gold medallist
(Montreal 1976)

'We went out there as a team and believed we could win. Now I am an Olympic champion.'

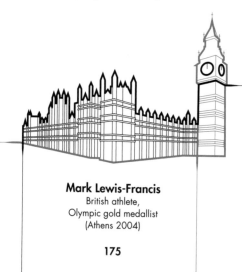

Mark Lewis-Francis
British athlete,
Olympic gold medallist
(Athens 2004)

175

'London has what it takes to host the greatest sporting show on earth.'

Bradley Wiggins
British cyclist, three-time Olympic gold
medallist (Athens 2004, Beijing 2008)

176

'You have to expect
things of yourself before
you can do them.'

Michael Jordan
American basketball player, two-time Olympic gold
medallist (Los Angeles 1984, Barcelona 1992)

'It was beyond skills almost,
it was so primeval. It was
just auto-pilot. We were
flying blind, rowing blind,
we rowed from the heart.'

Steve Williams
British rower, two-time Olympic gold
medallist (Athens 2004, Beijing 2008)

'If you fail to prepare, you're prepared to fail.'

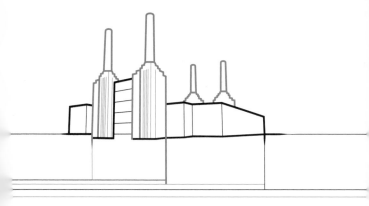

Mark Spitz
American swimmer, nine-time Olympic gold
medallist (Mexico 1968, Munich 1972)

'Through everything I've gone through ... I never gave up my dream of winning a gold medal in the Olympics.'

Dan O'Brien
American athlete,
Olympic gold medallist
(Atlanta 1996)

180

'Winning the gold medal was undoubtedly the biggest day of my career, mostly because I won the way I had prepared to run it. It was a totally satisfying experience.'

Frank Shorter
American athlete, Olympic gold medallist
(Munich 1972)

'When the sun is shining I can do anything, no mountain is too high, no trouble too difficult to overcome.'

Wilma Rudolph
American athlete, three-time Olympic gold medallist (Rome 1960)

'We only have two things that we share in this life, we are born and we die. And what we do in between those times, we've got to be happy. I don't let the outside world deter me.'

Dawn Fraser
Australian swimmer, four-time
Olympic gold medallist (Melbourne 1956,
Rome 1960, Tokyo 1964)

'If you win something and you haven't put everything into it, you haven't actually achieved anything at all. When you've had to work hard for something and you've got the best you can out of yourself on that given day, that's where you get satisfaction from.'

Ian Thorpe
Australian swimmer, five-time Olympic gold
medallist (Sydney 2000, Athens 2004)

'Athletics brings out a side of you that is wonderful. It brings out so many good attributes like competing, intensity and playing at the highest level.'

Julie Foudy
American footballer, two-time
Olympic gold medallist
(Atlanta 1996, Athens 2004)

'My mother said believe in yourself and believe in your dreams. I took away those words and will keep them in my memory for a lifetime.'

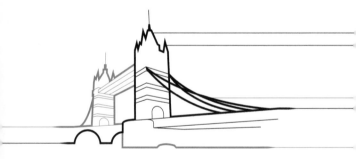

Dominique Dawes
American gymnast, Olympic gold medallist
(Atlanta 1996)

'Champions aren't made in the gyms. Champions are made from something they have deep inside them – a desire, a dream, a vision.'

Cassius Clay
American boxer, Olympic gold medallist
(Rome 1960)

'I am a member of a team,
and I rely on the team, I
defer to it and sacrifice
for it, because the team,
not the individual, is the
ultimate champion.'

Mia Hamm
American footballer, two-time Olympic gold
medallist (Atlanta 1996, Athens 2004)

188

'Believe in yourself, not only in swimming, but in life itself. You always have to have fun. You have to have an open mind. If you're not enjoying it, don't do it. Life's too short.'

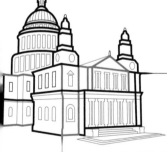

Debbie Meyer
American swimmer, three-time Olympic
gold medallist (Mexico 1968)

'There are hurdles to overcome in sport and in life. Sport is a very valuable learning ground for how to live your life in the best possible way.'

Lynn Davies
British athlete, Olympic gold medallist
(Tokyo 1964)

'No negative thoughts cross my mind on race day. When I look into their eyes, I know I'm going to beat them.'

Danny Harris
American athlete,
Olympic silver medallist
(Los Angeles 1984)

191

'Keep your dreams alive.
Understand to achieve anything
requires faith and belief in
yourself, vision, hard work,
determination, and dedication.
Remember all things are possible
for those who believe.'

Gail Devers
American athlete, three-time Olympic gold medallist
(Barcelona 1992, Atlanta 1996)